P9-DOG-700

Awesome Science

A CHAPTER BOOK

BY KATHERINE GLEASON

children's press®

A Division of Scholastic Inc.
New York Toronto London Auckland Sydney
Mexico City New Delhi Hong Kong
Danbury, Connecticut

For Ann Marie and Mega

ACKNOWLEDGMENTS

The author would like to thank all the scientists whose exciting work has made this book possible. In particular, thanks and best wishes go to Dr. Donald Colgan, Principal Research Scientist, Australian Museum, Sydney, Australia; Dana Jones, Personal Assistant to the Director, Australian Museum; Dr. Michael Archer, Dean of Science at the University of New South Wales; Dr. Jeffrey Friedman of the Howard Hughes Medical Institute at Rockefeller University; and Dr. Pamela Rosenthal of New York City.

Library of Congress Cataloging-in-Publication Data

Gleason, Katherine.
    Awesome science : a chapter book / by Katherine Gleason.
        p. cm.—(True tales)
Includes bibliographical references and index.
    ISBN 0-516-23727-6 (lib. bdg.)   0-516-24681-X (pbk.)
    1. Genetics—Juvenile literature.   I. Title. II. Series.

QH437.5.G56 2004
576.5—dc22
                                2004000416

CONTENTS

American
Scientific
Products

INTRODUCTION

In labs all over the world, there are scientists who are looking inside the cells of living things. A cell is very small. Your body, for example, contains trillions of cells. So imagine how small something would have to be to fit inside a cell! Even though it is tiny, the stuff inside your cells is important.

In 1953, James Watson and Francis Crick figured out one of the secrets of life, and they found the answer inside a cell. Their findings paved the way for many important discoveries in **genetics**. Jeffrey Friedman and his team of scientists used genetics to discover why some mice grow to be very fat. In Scotland, Ian Wilmut used genetics to create a sheep named Dolly. Michael Archer wants to use genetics to bring a dead animal back to life.

Meet these scientists and learn about the important work they do.

CHAPTER ONE

DNA: THE SECRET OF LIFE

In 1953, James Watson cut a shape from a piece of cardboard. James was a scientist. The cardboard shape was one part of a model. James and his partner Francis Crick were figuring out how the shape fit together with the other shapes James had made. The two scientists were trying to build a model of **DNA**.

**Francis
Crick**

**James
Watson**

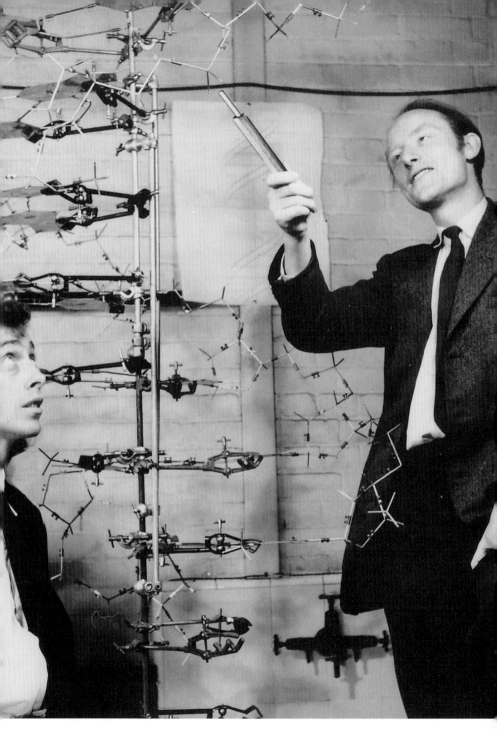

James Watson (left) and Francis Crick (right) with their model of DNA

DNA is short for deoxyribonucleic (dee-OX-ee-rye-bow-new-CLAY-ic) acid. DNA is an important part of all living cells. A cell is the basic building block of life. DNA is important because it tells the cells how to grow. DNA even gives the cells directions on how to make new cells.

The DNA in your cells sets the color of your eyes, the size of your feet, and the curliness or straightness of your hair. DNA is the basic building block that makes you the unique person that you are. You share some of your DNA with other people. That part of DNA makes us human.

DNA determines what you look like.

These identical twins share the same DNA.

You share some of your DNA with the people in your family, too. However, unless you are an **identical twin**, no one has the exact same DNA as you.

For centuries, scientists had wanted to know why children look like their parents. How are **traits**, such as eye color, passed down from parent to child? Why do some people have brown eyes and some people have blue eyes? By the 1950s scientists known as **geneticists** had found many answers. However, they still had lots of questions.

James and Francis knew that DNA was the thing that caused traits to pass from one generation to the next. They did not know how DNA did this important job. They hoped that their model would help them understand DNA better.

James Watson had been interested in DNA for many years. Born in Chicago in 1928, James finished college when he was only nineteen years old. After college, he studied in Indiana and then went to Cambridge, England, to learn more about DNA. At the lab in Cambridge, James met Francis Crick. The two scientists started working together.

Francis Crick was born in Northampton, England, in 1916. He studied physics and worked for the army during World War II. After the war, he went to Cambridge to study biology.

James and Francis put together many clues about DNA that other scientists had

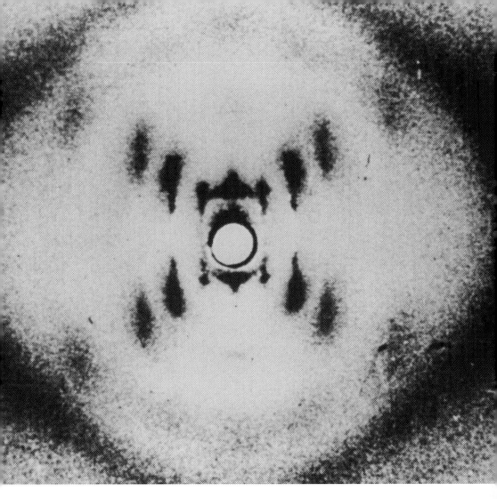

Rosalind Franklin took this X-ray photograph of DNA in 1953.

found. They studied what it was made of. They also studied a special type of X-ray photograph made by scientists Rosalind Franklin and Maurice Wilkins.

Rosalind Franklin

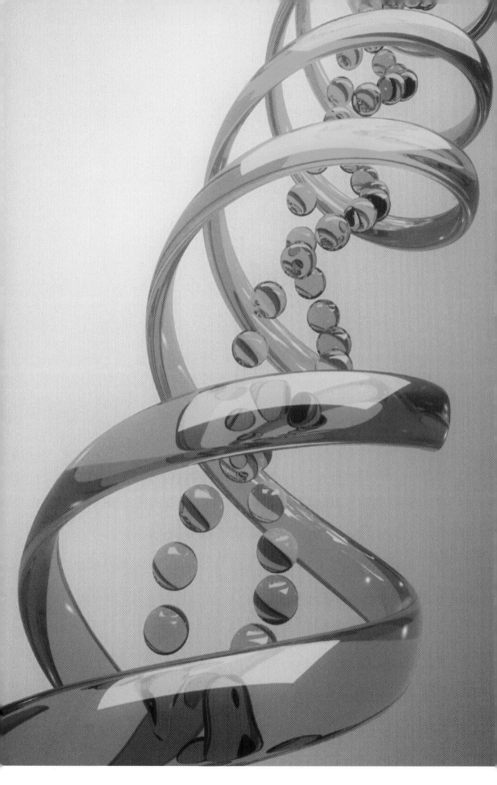

A computer model of DNA

DNA was too small to see, so scientists like Rosalind and Maurice used X-rays to try to learn more about what DNA looked like. Unlike an ordinary photograph, these fuzzy pictures show the pattern of X-rays that bounce off of DNA. Based on the patterns, specially trained scientists could make a good guess about the shape of DNA.

One Saturday morning, James and Francis realized they had found the answer. DNA looked like a spiral-shaped ladder. This shape became known as the "**double helix**." Helix means spiral.

The rungs of the ladder are made of four different **chemicals**. Each rung is made of two chemicals that form a pair. Once the scientists saw the shape of DNA, they understood how DNA made copies of itself so that new cells could grow.

When it is time for DNA to copy itself, the chemical pairs unzip down the middle.

James Watson (far right) receiving the Nobel Prize for Medicine

Then DNA looks like half a ladder with little half rungs. Each chemical rung then joins up with a new pair. This way a new ladder is formed.

James and Francis were excited by their discovery. At lunch that day, James told everyone that they had found "the secret of life."

In 1962, James Watson, Francis Crick, and Maurice Wilkins were given the Nobel Prize for their important work on DNA. Sadly, Rosalind Franklin had died in 1958, and so did not get to share this important award.

Francis Crick and James Watson's work on DNA has brought about many important discoveries in genetics.

CHAPTER TWO

FIGHTING FAT

The mouse waddled slowly across the cage toward its food. It could not move its bulky body fast. This mouse weighed more than twice as much as an ordinary mouse.

Doctor Jeffrey M. Friedman of the Howard Hughes Medical Institute at Rockefeller University studies **obese** (oh-BEESS) mice. A mouse that is obese is very, very fat. Jeffrey studies why these mice eat so much and grow so big.

Jeffrey Friedman

A scientist studies the patterns of DNA.

In 1994, Jeffrey made an important discovery. He looked at the DNA of obese mice. He found a **gene** that may make these mice fat. Scientists call sections of DNA genes. Each gene tells a body part to grow and work a certain way. For example, you have genes that tell your body the color of your eyes. You also have genes that help to determine how tall you will be. The gene that Jeffrey found in the obese mice is called "ob" for obesity.

In the lab, Jeffrey **cloned** the ob gene. This means that he made many copies of this section of DNA. Once he had lots of copies of the gene, he could start learning how the gene worked. Jeffrey spent eight years looking for, copying, and studying the ob gene.

Genes help to make **proteins**, which are important chemicals. Proteins get things done. Proteins help to build your body. Normally, the ob gene tells the fat in the body to make a protein called **leptin**.

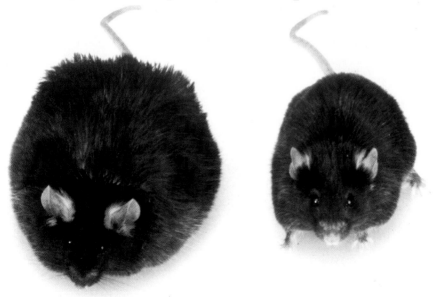

The mouse on the left carries an ob gene that does not make leptin.

Leptin helps to tell the body how much fat to store. Leptin also tells mice when to stop eating. Sometimes the gene doesn't do its job.

Jeffrey studied some mice that had something wrong with their ob gene. In these mice, the gene does not make leptin. Because they have no leptin, the mice eat and eat. They grow fatter and fatter. Eventually, they become obese. Jeffrey tried

The mouse on the right weighs more than the two mice on the left.

Scientists are trying to find out how leptin works in people.

giving some obese mice leptin. Very quickly, the mice began to eat less, and they became thinner.

Jeffrey also studies people. He found out that humans have a similar ob gene. Jeffrey cloned the ob gene in people. He discovered that the human ob gene is put together in much the same way as the mouse ob gene. In people, this gene makes a human version of leptin.

Jeffrey wanted to find out how similar human leptin is to mouse leptin. He tried giving human leptin to mice. The mice lost weight just as they did when they were given mouse leptin. Jeffrey and the other scientists in his lab want to learn how the ob gene works in humans. They also want to learn all about human leptin. They hope that doctors may be able to use leptin to help people who are obese.

Obesity in humans is not always caused by genes alone. Poor diet and lack of exercise can also make people obese. Obesity in humans can cause many health problems. Some obese people suffer from high blood pressure. Others get heart disease. These health problems can be very serious and may even lead to death. Jeffrey and other scientists hope that their work will help all people live longer and healthier lives.

It is important to eat right and exercise in order to stay healthy.

CHAPTER THREE

THE MOST FAMOUS SHEEP IN THE WORLD

The scientist watched as Dolly, a very special sheep, munched on some grass. Dolly raised her head and looked at her lambs. Her lambs ate grass next to her.

Dolly the sheep was born in July 1996. Ian Wilmut and the other scientists at the Roslin Institute in Scotland were very proud of Dolly. They were proud because they created Dolly in the lab. Dolly was a clone.

Ian Wilmut

An animal that is a clone is an exact genetic copy of another animal. Dolly shared the same DNA with another sheep. Even though she was older than Dolly, you can think of this other sheep as Dolly's genetic twin. Dolly and her twin have the same DNA, but they are not exactly the same. They have had different experiences. They have eaten different food, played in different fields, and slept in different barns. So, Dolly and her genetic twin are not exactly alike.

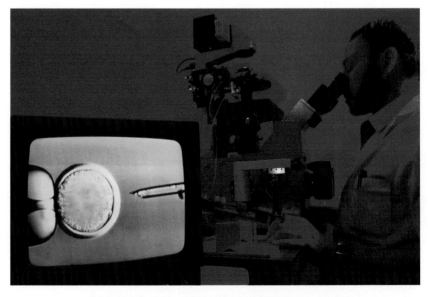

A scientist uses a microscopic needle to remove DNA from a cell.

Dolly was the first **mammal** to be cloned from an adult animal. To make Dolly, Ian Wilmut and the other scientists took a cell from Dolly's genetic twin. The twin sheep was six years old at the time. The cell that they used came from her **udder**.

In the lab, the scientists removed the DNA from the twin sheep's udder cell **(1)**. They used a **microscopic** needle to do this. The scientists then took an egg cell out of a second sheep **(2)**. Using another needle, they removed the DNA from the egg. Then they put the DNA from the udder cell into the egg **(3)**. Finally they placed the egg with its new DNA into the **womb** (WOOM) of a third sheep **(4)**.

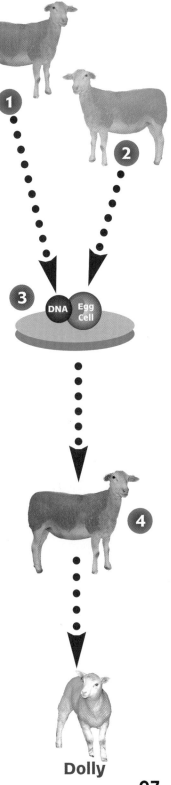

Dolly

27

The scientists were not sure if their experiment would work. In fact, they tried 277 times! That means that they used 277 eggs and put the DNA from 277 udder cells inside of them. They let the eggs with their new DNA grow for six days. Only twenty-nine of the eggs grew and developed normally. Scientists placed each of these eggs inside a sheep to grow more. One of the eggs grew and grew. This time the scientists were successful. About twenty-one weeks later, Dolly was born.

Dolly as a lamb with her birth mother

Usually the DNA of an udder cell makes other udder cells. To make Dolly, the DNA from the udder cell needed to change. Scientists think that the move into the egg changed the udder cell DNA. Once in the egg, the DNA made skin and muscle and brain cells. Eventually, it made all of the cells in a sheep's body.

The scientists did not tell people about Dolly right away. They wanted to make sure she was normal and healthy first. In February 1997, the scientists told the world about Dolly. Dolly's story landed on the front page of newspapers.

Photographers came from all over the world to take Dolly's picture.

Everyone wanted to know about Dolly. She was even invited to appear on a talk show!

By the end of Dolly's first week in the spotlight, more than fifty photographers had taken her picture. More than 100 reporters had talked to the scientists, and more than sixteen film crews had filmed her. Seven-month-old Dolly became the most famous sheep in the world.

Dolly's birth was called one of the most important scientific breakthroughs of the 1990s. From their work with Dolly, scientists hope to learn how to make farm animals that are disease free. They are also using cloned animals to help people with serious diseases. For example, certain cloned sheep produce chemicals in their milk that can help people with some diseases.

Some people think that cloning animals is wrong. They are afraid scientists might create a monster by mistake. Other people think that using animals in experiments is wrong because the animals could be hurt.

In Germany, people wearing sheep masks protest animal cloning.

Dolly grew up to be a mother herself. She had four lambs during her life. She even had a sweater made from her wool. The blue and white sweater was designed by a thirteen-year-old girl named Holly Wharton. On the front, the sweater shows Dolly in a green field. The sweater is on display in the "Making the Modern World" gallery at the Science Museum in London, England.

Dolly with Bonnie, her first lamb

Holly Wharton designed this sweater made from Dolly's wool.

Unfortunately, Dolly died young. Sheep usually live to be eleven or twelve years old. Dolly died at age six. After she died, scientists found that Dolly had a lung disease and **arthritis** (ar-THRYE-tiss). Both of these diseases are usually found in older sheep.

Some people think Dolly might have gotten sick because she was a clone. They think that Dolly's DNA was already old. Remember that Dolly's DNA came from a six-year-old sheep. So, by the time Dolly reached the age of six, her DNA was twelve. Most scientists think that they still don't know enough about clones to know why Dolly got sick. They want to keep working and learn more.

Dolly's body has been stuffed. You can see it at the Royal Museum in Edinburgh, Scotland.

Ian Wilmut stands next to Dolly's stuffed body.

CHAPTER FOUR

BACK TO LIFE

A large dog-like animal with stripes across its back paces in its cage. It raises its narrow snout, as if sniffing the air. It opens its powerful jaws. Inside are forty-six sharp teeth. It rises up on its hind legs. Then the image of this beautiful creature flickers and fades. It is only a movie.

After she died, scientists discovered that Benjamin was really a female.

Several old movies show pictures of **thylacines** (THY-lah-sines). The last known thylacine was named Benjamin. Benjamin died in a zoo in Hobart, Australia, on September 7, 1936.

Thylacines are **extinct** (ek-STINGKT), which means that there are no living ones left.

Thylacines used to live in Tasmania (taz-MAY-knee-a), an island near Australia. This animal is also called the Tasmanian tiger or Tasmanian wolf. Unfortunately, people thought that thylacines would hurt their sheep and chickens. So, they hunted and killed them. In fact, thylacines rarely ate chickens or sheep. They ate other birds, small kangaroos, and mice.

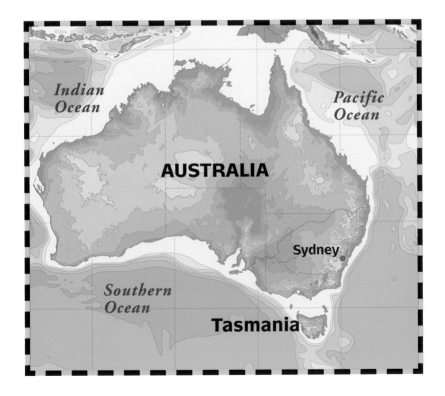

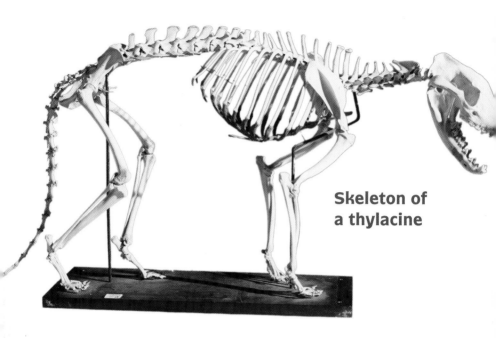

Skeleton of a thylacine

Michael Archer, the former director of the Australian Museum in Sydney, has been interested in thylacines for more than thirty years. He wants to bring the extinct thylacine back to life.

The museum owns a few dead thylacines. One baby thylacine has been kept in a jar. The jar is full of **alcohol** (AL-kuh-hol) to keep the thylacine from rotting. This dead thylacine has been in a jar since 1866.

Scientists at the museum want to try to

clone a living thylacine by using the DNA of the dead ones. Some people think that this can never be done. The scientists know that it will be hard work. They also know they might not succeed. They have decided to try anyway.

The scientists started working to collect DNA from the preserved baby thylacine.

Michael Archer studies a preserved baby thylacine.

They hoped that the alcohol had helped to keep the thylacine's DNA in good condition. They worried that the DNA might be broken up into pieces that were too small for them to use.

So far, the scientists have been lucky. In 1999, they looked at some samples of thylacine muscle, **bone marrow**, heart, and liver in the lab. They discovered that these samples still contained good DNA. They took DNA out of the samples and examined it. They needed to learn exactly how thylacine DNA is put together.

In 2002, they were able to copy some of the thylacine's DNA in the lab. They hope to copy all of the DNA. Copying all of it could take years. Once they have

A drawing of a thylacine

The Tasmanian devil is a close relative of the thylacine.

done that, they will try to clone a thylacine.
To do this, they will put its DNA inside the
egg cell of another animal. They will use
one of the thylacine's close relatives,
probably a **Tasmanian devil**. Many
scientists think that this will be hard to do.
That's because Tasmanian devils are fairly
different from thylacines. Some of the

scientists involved think that they may be able to recreate the thylacine by the year 2010. Others think it will take a lot longer.

Some people think that cloning a thylacine is impossible. Some think that trying is just a waste of time and money. Other people think that trying to bring an extinct animal back to life is wrong.

Michael Archer says it was wrong for people in the past to hunt and kill thylacines. If we could bring the thylacine back to life, it would help undo the wrong done in the past. He is willing to work hard to bring these animals back to life. He is determined to see a living thylacine during his lifetime.

Maybe one day thylacines will be seen in the wild instead of in museums.

GLOSSARY

alcohol (AL-kuh-hol) a clear liquid used in certain drinks, medicines, and as a preservative

arthritis (ar-THRYE-tiss) a disease in which the body's joints become swollen and painful

bone marrow soft stuff found inside the bones

chemical something of weight that takes up space and is used in chemistry

clone to copy a living thing by copying its DNA; an exact genetic copy of a living thing

DNA (deoxyribonucleic acid) (dee-OX-ee-rye-bow-new-CLAY-ic) a long chain of information that fits inside the cells of all living things

double helix a spiral of DNA that has two strands of genetic material

extinct (ek-STINGKT) having no living examples left

gene lengths of DNA that tell the body how to grow and to work

geneticist someone who studies genes and how traits are passed down

genetics the study of genes and how traits are passed down

identical twin a twin with the exact same genes as his or her twin

leptin a protein that controls the way fat is stored in the body

mammal an animal that keeps its body temperature the same. Mammals have fur and feed milk to their young.

microscopic something so small that it can only be seen under a microscope

obese (oh-BEESS) very, very fat

protein a chemical that animals and people need to grow and to fix things in the body

Tasmanian devil a meat-eating animal with black and white fur and a long tail

thylacine (THY-lah-sine) a meat-eating animal that looked like a wolf, but had stripes like a tiger and a pouch like a kangaroo

trait a thing—such as hair color, eye color, or height—that helps to make you who you are

udder the bag-like part of cows, sheep, and goats where milk comes from

womb (WOOM) the place inside the body where babies grow

FIND OUT MORE

DNA: The Secret of Life
http://ology.amnh.org/genetics/index.html
Learn more about genetics, DNA, and some of the basic puzzles of all life.

Fighting Fat
http://whyfiles.org/051fat_fixes/leptin.html
Read about ongoing research on leptin and its role in humans.

The Most Famous Sheep in the World
http://www.sciencemuseum.org.uk/antenna/dolly/
Learn more about Dolly and post your opinion on cloning.

Back to Life
http://www.naturalworlds.org/thylacine/
See old movies of thylacines living in a zoo.

More Books to Read

Have a Nice DNA (Enjoy Your Cells, 3) by Fran Balkwill and Mic Rolph, Cold Spring Harbor Laboratory Press, 2002

Eyewitness: Life (Eyewitness Books) by David Burnie, DK Publishing, 2000

Ingenious Genes: Microexplorers: Learning About the Fantastic Skills of Genetic Engineers and Watching Them at Work (Microexplorers Series) by Norbert Landa, Patrick A. Baeuerle, Barrons Juveniles, 1998

Baa!: The Most Interesting Book You'll Ever Read About Genes and Cloning (Mysterious You) by Cynthia Pratt Nicolson, Kids Can Press, 2001

INDEX

PHOTO CREDITS

MEET THE AUTHOR

Katherine Gleason has worked in children's publishing as an editor, project manager, and author. She has written numerous books for children and a few for adults, as well. She particularly enjoys writing and reading books about animals, ancient cultures, and faraway places. Her love of travel has taken her all over the world, and she has, in fact, visited all seven of the Earth's continents. Gleason lives in New York City with her cat, Elphaba.